A Month's Journey with St. Patrick

A Month's Journey with St. Patrick

CONTAINING AN INSPIRATIONAL QUOTE, A REFLECTION, AND A PRAYER

By
FR. NEIL XAVIER O'DONOGHUE

Illustrated

CATHOLIC BOOK PUBLISHING CORP.
New Jersey

NIHIL OBSTAT: Fr. Philip-Michael F. Tangorra, S.T.L.
Censor Librorum

IMPRIMATUR: ✠ Most Rev. Arthur J. Serratelli, S.T.D., S.S.L., D.D.
Bishop of Paterson

May 5, 2017

The Nihil Obstat and Imprimatur are official declarations that a book or a pamphlet is free of doctrinal or moral error. No implication is contained therein that those who have granted the Nihil Obstat and Imprimatur agree with the contents, opinions, or statements expressed.

(T-53)

ISBN 978-1-941243-95-4

Printed in the U.S.A.
www.catholicbookpublishing.com

I, PATRICK, am a sinner, the most uncultured and smallest among all the faithful, indeed many people consider me to be worthless.

—Confessio 1

MAR. 1

REFLECTION. Christianity is a religion which treasures humility. All of us are called to be humble and it is a struggle for most of us.

Jesus tells us that "everyone who exalts himself will be humbled, and the one who humbles himself will be exalted" (Lk 14:11).

PRAYER. *Lord, grant me true discernment of my own self-worth and dignity, but never let me condemn myself or others as worthless. I ask this through the invocation of the Trinity. Amen.*

THE Lord revealed to me my sense of unbelief so that I could repent of my sins and turn with my whole heart to the Lord my God. God looked at my misery and had mercy upon my youth and ignorance . . . He had compassion for me.

—Confessio 2

MAR. 2

REFLECTION. We all doubt and question our faith at times. St. Patrick had a life filled with difficulties. But his faith in Christ was to triumph, and God gave him the gift of perseverance in the midst of many problems.

God is also very present in our lives today and every day invites us to come to Him again.

PRAYER. *Lord, my faith is weak; help my disbelief. Lead me by Your light of faith. I ask this through the invocation of the Trinity. Amen.*

MAR. 3

I CANNOT be silent . . . about all the gifts and graces that the Lord in His mercy bestowed upon me . . . [because] we must praise Him and tell of His marvels to every nation under the heavens. —*Confessio* 3

REFLECTION. We are usually very quick to ask God for help, but how good are we at thanking Him afterward?

Gratitude and praise of God go hand in hand. By being grateful and generous we become more like Our Lord in our everyday lives.

PRAYER. *Lord, help me to see how You have answered my prayers; give me the gift of praise and the courage to share the story of Your goodness with others. I ask this through the invocation of the Trinity. Amen.*

MAR. 4

THE Holy Spirit makes believers and those who obey God into children of God and coheirs of Christ as we confess and adore the one God in the Trinity of holy Names. —*Confessio* 4

REFLECTION. Our faith is founded on the blessed Trinity. God is a communion of persons; He lives together as Father, Son, and Holy Spirit.

By becoming coheirs with Christ we are granted entrance into this divine life.

PRAYER. *O God, give me the grace of entering into the divine trinitarian life that Your Son won for me by His Cross and Resurrection and gave me through His Holy Spirit. I ask this through the invocation of the Trinity. Amen.*

MAR. 5

GOD Himself has said through the prophet: Call on Me in the day of your tribulation and I will free you and you will proclaim My greatness.

—*Confessio* 5

REFLECTION. Christianity is a personal meeting with the love of God that we must proclaim from the housetops. We cannot take our faith and hide it under a bushel basket.

We don't share our faith to please God; we do it because it will be good both for ourselves and our listeners.

PRAYER. *Heavenly Father, grant me the grace of gratitude. Allow me to glorify Your name with my lips and with my life. I ask this through the invocation of the Trinity. Amen.*

MAR. 6

UNLIKE the others I did not study law and the sacred sciences in an excellent balance. These men, unlike me, were not obliged to change their language in their youth, but were able to perfect their native tongue. —*Confessio* 9

REFLECTION. Because Patrick was kidnapped as a young man and brought as a slave to Ireland, he could not complete his schooling.

Yet, in spite of everything, God was able to do great things in him, for His "power is made perfect in weakness" (2 Cor 12:9).

PRAYER. *Lord, help me to look past my inadequacies, my weaknesses, and my past failures and to trust in Your power. I ask this through the invocation of the Trinity. Amen.*

MAR. 7

EVEN today I blush and am very embarrassed by my lack of learning. I am quite unable to express my story in the same way as those people who are well trained . . . and my words do not express exactly that which my spirit feels.

—Confessio 10

REFLECTION. Patrick never overcame his sense of inadequacy. He always felt that he would have been a better missionary if he had finished school.

Yet, despite this he always did what he thought God wanted him to do.

PRAYER. *Lord, give me the grace of perseverance. In spite of my inadequacies allow me to serve You. I ask this through the invocation of the Trinity. Amen.*

MAR. 8

WE ARE a letter written by Christ. . . . Although this letter may not be refined it is very strong and true, written in your hearts not with ink but with the Spirit of the living God.

—Confessio 11

REFLECTION. Christ gives us strength to bring salvation to others. What matters is not our personal talents, but whether we allow our hearts to be inscribed with the words of salvation.

If we are true to Christ's message we will truly be close to the living God.

PRAYER. *Lord, may I be an instrument of Your peace in this generation. I ask this through the invocation of the Trinity. Amen.*

THE Strong One came and in His mercy He took me out and He lifted me on high and placed me on the top of His wall. Therefore, I must cry aloud in thanksgiving to the Lord.

MAR. 9

—*Confessio* 12

REFLECTION. In His mercy God has chosen us. He raises the weak and the lowly and gives them places of honor in His Church.

But we must never forget that all honor belongs to God and that we are only "unprofitable servants" (Lk 17:10).

PRAYER. *Lord, give me the gift of humility so that I may never think that I can earn salvation without You. I ask this through the invocation of the Trinity. Amen.*

AFTER so many calamities and disasters and after many years of slavery among these people, the Lord has given me so many more graces than I could even have imagined in my youth.

MAR. 10

—*Confessio* 15

REFLECTION. God is generous with His grace. He always surpasses our expectations.

Even after many years of slavery, Patrick can see how God does "all things well" (Mk 7:37).

PRAYER. *Lord, help me not to give up in times of disaster and calamity. Give me the patience I need to see how You work through all aspects of my life for my benefit and that of those around me. I ask this through the invocation of the Trinity. Amen.*

MAR. 11

WHEN I came to Ireland I spent each day tending sheep and I prayed many times during the day. . . . When I was tending the sheep on mountains and in woods . . . I would awaken and pray in the snow, in the frost and in the rain.
—*Confessio* 16

REFLECTION. During his years of slavery, Patrick learned to pray. He prayed one hundred times a day and as many again at night.

This was to be the bedrock of his faith.

PRAYER. *Lord, grant me the gift of perseverance in prayer. May I cast all my cares upon You aware that You want the best for me. I ask this through the invocation of the Trinity. Amen.*

MAR. 12

CONVERT and turn with your whole heart to the Lord my God, for nothing is impossible to Him. —*Confessio* 19

REFLECTION. We worry about so many things, but we often forget that God is our heavenly Father Who provides for us in times of trouble.

The Lord never abandoned Patrick. After this he always encouraged others to turn to the Lord.

PRAYER. *Lord, may I repent of my sins and obtain Your forgiveness. I ask You to provide for me in this life and to bring me to heaven in the next. I pray especially that I may never doubt Your love. I ask this through the invocation of the Trinity. Amen.*

SATAN tempted me. This temptation was stronger than I ever experienced. . . . I started calling out at the top of my voice, . . . immediately all the weight left me. Christ Jesus came to my aid.

MAR. 13

—Confessio 20

REFLECTION. If we want to be disciples of Christ we will face challenges. Evil exists in our world and each of us is tempted by it. Sometimes we give up hope.

But if we call on the Lord, He will send us His help. He is merciful and is always ready to welcome us back.

PRAYER. *Father, You are rich in mercy. May I never doubt Your love. Help me to lead a virtuous life. I ask this through the invocation of the Trinity. Amen.*

ONE night as if in a vision I saw a man come from Ireland . . . it was as if he was bringing thousands of letters to me.

MAR. 14

—Confessio 23

REFLECTION. After Patrick escaped from slavery, he felt obliged to go back to the land of his captivity and share the Good News with his former captors.

How do I act toward those who have hurt me? Do I pray for the grace of forgiveness?

PRAYER. *Lord, never let me be consumed by hatred. Banish all evil from my heart. May I love others as You have loved me. I ask this through the invocation of the Trinity. Amen.*

MAR. 15

I WAS tested by some of my elders who came to me and said that I was not fit to fulfill a bishop's ministry. . . . But the Lord . . . helped me greatly in this trial.

—*Confessio* 26

REFLECTION. Before Patrick returned to Ireland as a missionary, some thought he was unworthy. But God protected Patrick.

We too are unworthy, yet the Lord always uses "earthen vessels" to carry the treasures of His Gospel (2 Cor 4:7).

PRAYER. *Lord, I know that I am not worthy to be Your disciple. Help me to follow You more closely and always keep my eyes fixed upon Your goodness. I ask this through the invocation of the Trinity. Amen.*

MAR. 16

TOMORROW we will remember St. Patrick. May his faith in Christ the Savior sustain you . . . at the most difficult times; and may his missionary devotion remind you . . . of the importance of Christian education for your children.

—Pope Francis, March 16, 2016

REFLECTION. Patrick's message is valid for all peoples and all times. We all need to come to meet Christ.

If we are inspired by Him, God will be with us at all times and bring us to His Kingdom.

PRAYER. *Lord, may I turn to You when I am sick and when I am joyful, when I am poor and when I am rich. I ask this through the invocation of the Trinity. Amen.*

I GIVE thanks to the One who strengthens me in all things. . . . I felt a great strength from Him so that my good faith was approved in the sight of God and men. —*Confessio* 30

MAR. 17

REFLECTION. Even though Patrick had to face many challenges, God strengthened him so that he could meet them.

God will also strengthen us to carry out the good works that He has fashioned for us.

PRAYER. *Lord, give me the strength I need to do Your will, and in my weakness may Your glory be shown to those around me. I ask this through the invocation of the Trinity. Amen.*

INDEED I did not get to go to Ireland until these humiliations had nearly killed me. But this was providential for by this I was purified by the Lord. —*Confessio* 28

MAR. 18

REFLECTION. Patrick was able to be a great Saint, because God helped him to be humble. Pride is the mother of all other sins.

God allows us to see some of our sins, so that we may repent and be humble.

PRAYER. *Lord, make me humble. Do not allow me to be puffed up by pride. May I always see my own dignity and understand that everything good that I do has You as its inspiration and font. I ask this through the invocation of the Trinity. Amen.*

MAR. 19

I MUST not hide the gift of God that was generously bestowed on me in the land of my captivity. I looked hard for Him then and I found Him. *—Confessio* 33

REFLECTION. Patrick found Jesus in his missionary endeavors; he found the Lord in the place of his captivity.

Often when we look back at the difficult times in our lives, we can see how the goodness of the Lord accompanied us.

PRAYER. *Lord, help me to share my experience of You with those I meet. I pray that I may never give up on myself or others. Allow me to see Your footprints in my life. I ask this through the invocation of the Trinity. Amen.*

MAR. 20

TO THIS day I offer my soul to Him as a living sacrifice to Christ the Lord, for He has saved me from all my anguish. *—Confessio* 34

REFLECTION. The Lord does not want "sacrifice and offering" from us, but instead an open heart willing to do His will (see Ps 40:7, 9).

We all face anguish in our lives, but our hope and salvation come from our personal relationship with Christ.

PRAYER. *Lord, allow me to love You as a real person. I do not want to relate to You only out of fear or obligation. Grant that I may love You and trust You. I ask this through the invocation of the Trinity. Amen.*

W HY have You called me, O Lord? Why have You poured out so many divine graces upon me? So that today I can exalt and magnify Your name among the pagans in whatever place I find myself.

—Confessio 34

MAR. 21

REFLECTION. Despite his many hardships and tribulations, Patrick realized that God was good to him. This realization allowed him to praise God wherever he went and in whatever company he found himself.

Do we see God in our own lives? Do we praise Him at all times?

PRAYER. *Lord, penetrate me with Your goodness and allow my heart to praise You at all times. I ask this through the invocation of the Trinity. Amen.*

I AM more than ready to freely give my very life for the sake of His name. I want to pour out my life here until I die, if God be willing.

—Confessio 37

MAR. 22

REFLECTION. Although Patrick was not a martyr he experienced that he loved Jesus more than life itself.

Patrick's faith was not merely empty words and platitudes, but something strong enough to see him through the most difficult challenges.

PRAYER. *Lord, I want to believe in You and give myself to You, but so often I am stopped by my fears. Yet, You Lord can do great things in me. I ask this through the invocation of the Trinity. Amen.*

I WOULD love to visit my home and family. . . but I am tied by the Spirit Who protests to me that He would bear witness against me if I were to do this.

—*Confessio* 43

MAR. 23

REFLECTION. Sometimes the Holy Spirit inspires us to take a path that our loved ones cannot understand. Patrick learned to put God above everyone and everything else.

Do I need to ask God's grace to renounce my own comforts in order to announce His Kingdom?

PRAYER. *Lord, I am slow to believe in You, and I am too attached to life's comforts. Help me to put You first in my life. I ask this through the invocation of the Trinity. Amen.*

I WAS looking toward that eternal hope, and I was careful in all my affairs, so that no one could find me unfaithful nor could they find me ministering for the sake of earthly gain.

—*Confessio* 49

MAR. 24

REFLECTION. Discipleship always has the temptation of self-gain. Patrick took care to avoid discrediting the Gospel by taking any payment for himself.

Do we give freely what we have freely received (see Mt 10:8)?

PRAYER. *Lord, help me to love You for love's sake. May You be my greatest treasure. May this love prepare me for heaven and allow me to taste its goodness during my earthly pilgrimage. I ask this through the invocation of the Trinity. Amen.*

EVERY day I am expecting to be killed or robbed or reduced to slavery. But I do not fear because of the promise of heaven; indeed I throw myself into the hands of the all-powerful God Who controls everything. —*Confessio* 55

MAR. 25

REFLECTION. Patrick's faith was the refuge of his life. He faced innumerable challenges and difficulties, but he threw himself into God's hands.

Do I try to solve all of my problems by myself or do I allow the Lord to help me?

PRAYER. *Lord, help me to turn to You in times of tribulation and persecution. May I never lose hope, but may the promise of heaven inspire me. I ask this through the invocation of the Trinity. Amen.*

NOW I entrust my life to God Who is most faithful to me, and Whose ambassador I am in my unworthiness. —*Confessio* 56

MAR. 26

REFLECTION. An ambassador does not stand for himself; he represents someone else. Patrick knew that he was representing God. Therefore he did not trust in his own resources, but placed all of his trust in God.

Who do I trust in?

PRAYER. *God, I thank You for calling me to be a member of Your Church and of Your holy people. Help me to be a worthy ambassador for You and to serve You faithfully. I ask this through the invocation of the Trinity. Amen.*

MAR. 27

ANYONE who does the will of Christ will not perish but will remain forever. He will reign with the Father and the Holy Spirit, before time and now and for ages of ages. Amen. *—Confessio* 60

REFLECTION. Our faith is not only for this present life. We are destined for the Kingdom of God.

If we follow Christ we will not perish for eternity but have eternal life.

PRAYER. *Lord, help me to do Your holy will. Help me to live for heaven and not for things of this earth. May I live a life of Christian dignity and serve You all my days. I ask this through the invocation of the Trinity. Amen.*

MAR. 28

I DO not wish to say such hard and severe things, but I am compelled to speak by the zeal for God and I am urged by the truth of Christ. I am also urged by the love I have for my neighbors and children.

—Letter to Coroticus 1

REFLECTION. As a bishop Patrick loved the members of his flock and did his utmost to fight for their rights.

Do I speak out for the rights of the downtrodden? Do I lend my voice to the voiceless?

PRAYER. *Lord, open my eyes to see the needs of my fellow men and women. May I make their plights my own and help them in any way I can. I ask this through the invocation of the Trinity. Amen.*

MAR. 29

I MYSELF am not the source of that holy mercy which is offered through me to those people, people who once made a captive of me. —*Letter to Coroticus* 10

REFLECTION. We are not the Messiah and can never take Christ's place. Patrick knew his place in God's plan.

Do I allow God to do His work or do I stand in His way?

PRAYER. *Lord, help me to trust You and may Your holy mercy flow through me to those who are most in need of it. May I always glorify You with both my lips and actions. I ask this through the invocation of the Trinity. Amen.*

MAR. 30

IT GIVES me great joy to stand here with you today . . . and to proclaim this same Jesus, the Incarnate Word of God, the Savior of the world. . . . May the light of Christ, the light of faith, continue always to shine out from Ireland. —St. John Paul II, September 29, 1979

REFLECTION. Jesus is the same "yesterday, today, and forever" (Heb 13:8), and the Church that Patrick helped found in Ireland will never die.

Our world is full of darkness, but the light of Christ is more powerful than the darkness.

PRAYER. *Lord, may Your light find a home in me. May I be penetrated by that light and may it radiate to those I meet. I ask this through the invocation of the Trinity. Amen.*

MAR. 31

MY MESSAGE to you today cannot be different from what Saint Patrick taught you. I preach what he preaches: Christ, Who is the "Prince of Peace," Who reconciled us to God and to each other, Who is the source of all unity.

—St. John Paul II, September 29, 1979

REFLECTION. The message of St. Patrick is as relevant today as it always has been.

It encourages us to meet the "Prince of Peace," to find forgiveness in Him, and to live a life of communion with our brothers and sisters in Christ.

PRAYER. *Lord, may I always cherish the Faith of my Fathers and share with others the beauty of knowing Christ. I ask this through the invocation of the Trinity. Amen.*

ST. PATRICK'S BREASTPLATE

I ARISE today
Through a mighty strength, the invocation of the Trinity,
Through belief in the Threeness,
Through confession of the Oneness
of the Creator of creation.

I arise today
Through the strength of Christ's birth with His baptism,
Through the strength of His crucifixion with His burial,
Through the strength of His resurrection and His ascension,
Through the strength of His descent for the judgment of doom.

I arise today
Through the strength of the love of cherubim,
In the obedience of angels,
In the service of archangels,
In the hope of resurrection to meet with reward,
In the prayers of patriarchs,
In the predictions of prophets,

St. Patrick's Breastplate

In the preaching of apostles,
In the faith of confessors,
In the innocence of virgins,
In the deeds of righteous men.

I arise today, through
The strength of heaven,
The light of the sun,
The radiance of the moon,
The splendor of fire,
The speed of lightning,
The swiftness of wind,
The depth of the sea,
The stability of the earth,
The firmness of rock.

I arise today, through
God's strength to pilot me,
God's might to uphold me,
God's wisdom to guide me,
God's eye to look before me,
God's ear to hear me,
God's word to speak for me,
God's hand to guard me,
God's shield to protect me,

God's hosts to save me
From snares of the devil,
From temptation of vices,
From every one who desires me ill,
far and near, alone or in a multitude.

I summon today
All these powers between me and evil,
Against every cruel and merciless power
that may oppose my body and soul,
Against incantations of false prophets,
Against black laws of pagans,
Against false laws of heretics,
Against craft of idolatry,
Against spells of witches and smiths and wizards,
Against every knowledge that corrupts man's body and soul;

Christ to shield me today
Against poison, against burning,
Against drowning, against wounding,
So that there may come to me an abundance of reward.

Christ with me,
Christ before me,

St. Patrick's Breastplate

Christ behind me,
Christ in me,
Christ beneath me,
Christ above me,
Christ on my right,
Christ on my left,
Christ when I lie down,
Christ when I sit down,
Christ when I arise,
Christ in the heart of everyone who thinks of me,
Christ in the mouth of everyone who speaks of me,
Christ in every eye that sees me,
Christ in every ear that hears me.

PRAYER TO ST. PATRICK

APOSTLE sent by God to Ireland,
in your humility you called yourself a sinner,
but you became a most successful missionary
and prompted countless pagans
to follow the Savior.
Many of their descendants in turn
spread the Good News in numerous foreign lands.
Through your powerful intercession with God,
obtain the missionaries we need
to continue the work you began.

OFFICIAL MASS OF ST. PATRICK

Courtesy of the National Centre for Liturgy, St Patrick's College, Maynooth, Co. Kildare, Ireland.

Although St. Patrick's Day is only a commemoration in the General Roman Calendar and the* editio typica *of the Roman Missal just gives a Collect for the Mass, in Ireland this feast day is a solemnity. The Irish Episcopal Conference composed a full Mass for this day. The official texts of this Mass and the references to its Scripture readings are provided below. Although these texts are officially approved for use only in Ireland (and are not licit for liturgical use elsewhere), nonetheless the Church recognizes that all official prayer texts are a valid aid to personal prayer (see* Catechism of the Catholic Church, *1124). It is hoped that by providing them here they might serve as an additional source of prayer.

March 17

Saint Patrick, Bishop
Principal Patron of Ireland

Solemnity

Entrance Antiphon Gen 12:1-2

Go from your country and your kindred and your father's house to the land that I will show you. I will make of you a great nation, and I will bless you, and make your name great, so that you will be a blessing.

Collect

Lord, through the work of Saint Patrick in Ireland
we have come to acknowledge the mystery of the one true God
and give thanks for our salvation in Christ;
grant by his prayers
that we who celebrate this festival
may keep alive the fire of faith he kindled.
Through our Lord Jesus Christ, your Son,
who lives and reigns with you and the Holy Spirit,
one God, for ever and ever.

Readings: Year ABC

First Reading: Sirach (Eccles) 39:6-10

His memory will not disappear and his name will live through all generations.

Responsorial Psalm: Psalm 115:12-19. ℟. v. 12

Second Reading: 2 Timothy 4:1-8

Convince, rebuke and encourage, with the utmost patience in teaching.

Gospel Acclamation: James 1:21

Glory to you, O Christ, you are the Word of God!
Accept and submit to the word which has been planted in you and can save your souls.
Glory to you, O Christ, you are the Word of God!

Gospel Reading: Matthew 13:24-32

It is the smallest of all the seeds, but when it has grown it is the greatest of shrubs.

Year B ad libitum [optional]

First Reading: Jeremiah 1:4-9

You shall go to all to whom I send you.

Responsorial Psalm: Psalm 116. ℟. Mark 16:15

Response: Go out to the whole world: proclaim the Good News.

Second Reading: Romans 10:9-18

Faith comes from what is heard, through the Word of Christ.

Gospel Acclamation: Matthew 28:19-20

Glory to you, O Christ, you are the Word of God!
Go, make disciples of all nations, says the Lord; I am with you always, yes, to the end of time.

Glory to you, O Christ, you are the Word of God!

Gospel Reading: Mark 16:15-20

They went out and proclaimed the good news everywhere.

Year C ad libitum [optional]

First Reading: Amos 7:12-15

The Lord took me from following the flock.

Responsorial Psalm: Psalm 138:1-3, 7-10, 13-14. ℟. v. 9-10

Second Reading: 1 Thessalonians 2:2-8

We never came with words of flattery or with a pretext for greed.

Gospel Acclamation: Luke 4:18

Glory to you, O Christ, you are the Word of God!
The Lord has sent me to bring good news to the poor, to proclaim liberty to captives.
Glory to you, O Christ, you are the Word of God!

Gospel Reading: Luke 5:1-11

"Lord, I am a sinful man." Jesus said, "Do not be afraid."

Prayer over the Gifts

Lord, accept this pure sacrifice
which, through the labors of Saint Patrick,
your grateful people make
to the glory of your name.
Through Jesus Christ our Lord.

Preface

℣. The Lord be with you.
℟. And with your spirit.

℣. Lift up your hearts.
℟. We lift them up to the Lord.

℣. Let us give thanks to the Lord our God.
℟. It is right and just.

It is truly right and just, our duty and our salvation,
always and everywhere to give you thanks,
Lord, holy Father, almighty and eternal God,
and to proclaim your greatness with due praise
as we honor Saint Patrick.

For you drew him through daily prayer
in captivity and hardship
to know you as a loving Father.

You chose him out of all the world
to return to the land of his captors,
that they might acknowledge Jesus Christ, their Redeemer.

In the power of your Spirit you directed his paths
to win the sons and daughters of the Irish
to the service of the Triune God.

And so, with Angels and Archangels,
and with the great multitude of the Saints,
we sing the hymn of your praise, as without end we acclaim:

Holy, Holy, Holy…

Communion Antiphon Cf. Mt 8:11

Many will come from east and west
and sit down with Abraham, Isaac and Jacob
at the feast in the kingdom of heaven, says the Lord.

Prayer after Communion

Strengthen us, O Lord, by this sacrament
so that we may profess the faith taught by Saint Patrick
and proclaim it in our way of living.
Through Christ our Lord.

Solemn Blessing

May God the Father, who called us together
to celebrate the feast of Saint Patrick,
bless you, protect you, and keep you faithful.
℟. Amen.

May Christ the Lord, the High King of Heaven,
be near you at all times and shield you from evil.

℟. Amen.

May the Holy Spirit, who is the source of all holiness,
make you rich in the love of God's people.

℟. Amen.

And may the blessing of almighty God,
the Father, and the Son, ✠ and the Holy Spirit
come down on you and remain for ever.

℟. Amen.